Rad Sports

Kick Scooters
Techniques and Tricks

Aaron Rosenberg

the rosen publishing group's
rosen central

S

Published in 2003 by The Rosen Publishing Group, Inc.
29 East 21st Street, New York, NY 10010

First Edition

Library of Congress Cataloging-in-Publication Data

Rosenberg, Aaron.
Kick scooters techniques and tricks / by Aaron Rosenberg.— 1st ed.
    p. cm. — (Rad sports)
Summary: Discusses the history of kick or push scooters, choosing which one to buy, accessories and safety gear, and various kinds of tricks performed on a scooter.
Includes bibliographical references and index.
ISBN 0-8239-3846-8 (lib. bdg.)
1. Scooters—Juvenile literature. [1. Scooters.] I. Title. II.Series.
TL412 .R67 2003
796.6—dc21

2002007522

Manufactured in the United States of America

CONTENTS

Introduction

You've seen it on the street and on television—teens and kids whipping around a corner on a scooter. Maybe you asked, "A scooter? Weren't those the things my grandpa rode?" Well, your grandpa may indeed have had a scooter. These new scooters are different. They're sleek, portable, maneuverable, and very fast. They are kick scooters for the rad sports generation.

Lots of people have them, but most use them for commuting to work or school, or just for riding around the neighborhood with friends. You want a bit more, though, don't you? You want to leap and jump and spin, to show just what you and your scooter can do. Well, that's what we're going to talk about, from the basics of riding to rad tricks. So read on, and get ready to ride!

Chapter 1

The Kick Scooter

Why ride a kick scooter at all? Quite a few reasons, actually. First off, they're easy—simpler to control than a skateboard, easier to carry than a bike, and you don't have to take your shoes off, like you must to wear in-line skates. Scooters are also convenient—lots of people have them for short-range travel and can go up to ten miles per hour on a scooter.

Their portability makes them convenient as well—you can ride to school or work, fold up your scooter, and stick it in a locker or under a desk until you need it again. Riding a scooter is good exercise, since it relies on your muscles for movement. This also makes them environmentally friendly—no gas or oil to burn. The best reason to ride a scooter might just be because they're fun. No wonder more than five million were sold in the United States in their first year!

Definitions

The information in this book applies to all foldable muscle-powered scooters. The general term is "kick scooter" or "push scooter," since that's how you move (by kicking or pushing off from the ground with your foot).

Other types of scooters exist, of course. There are motorized scooters, which are exactly like kick scooters but with small motors in back. Then there are electric scooters, with bigger motors and (usually) seats—these look like small motorcycles. In this book we'll be dealing only with the kick scooter.

History

Kick scooters date back at least eighty years. Back then they were basically wood-and-metal skateboards with a vertical pole at the front end. These early scooters were wobbly and didn't go very fast. They were slow because of their metal or wood wheels. The skateboard replaced the scooter in the 1960s. Skateboards were smaller, faster, and could be used for doing tricks. By the 1970s, the scooter all but disappeared.

Then in 1998 a buyer from the store The Sharper Image saw a man at a Chicago sporting-goods trade show riding a scooter around the floor, but it was unlike anything

Kick scooters were popular way back in the 1920s. These young riders are at the starting line for a scooter race.

Richard Thalheimer *(pictured)* is the founder of The Sharper Image. His company was the first American retail firm to sell the modern kick scooter.

he'd seen before. This scooter was made from aluminum and rode on polyurethane (plastic) wheels (the same kind that brought renewed popularity to the skateboard). A hinge in the front allowed this scooter to fold into a small, light-weight package. The rider was Gino Tsai, a Taiwanese businessman, and his company, JD Corporation, pro-duced bicycle parts and electric scooters. JD licensed their new Razor Scooter to The Sharper Image for worldwide distribution. Suddenly, the wave of scooter pop-ularity had begun.

Since then, a number of other companies have produced their own versions of the kick scooter. Steve Patmont created Patmont Motor Werks in California, back in 1985, to pro-duce his patented motor scooter with foldable handles, which he dubbed the Go-Ped. After the Razor appeared, Patmont created a muscle-powered version of the Go-Ped, called the Know-Ped. Today, the Know-Ped is one of the most popular kick scooters on the market and has a very strong community of fans and enthusiasts.

Buying a Scooter

The first thing to think about when buying a kick scooter is what you'll use it for. Are you planning to ride to school or around the neighborhood at a leisurely pace, or do you want to do tricks and leaps with it? Some scooters are tougher, with more sturdy frames. These are made to handle tricks. Others are built for comfort and efficiency and should be used only for fun.

Price and Size

A simple, no-frills scooter will cost around $100. A high-end scooter with several added features can run closer to $400. It's a good idea to start with a cheaper model so that you can practice on it and see whether travel or tricks is what you want from a scooter.

Consider the size and weight of the scooter. Are you planning to carry it around with you? Then you'll want one that folds up into a smaller size and that's lighter in weight. Some kick scooters weigh as little as 6 pounds (2.5 kilograms), while others are closer to 12 (5 kg). That's a big difference. The board can also vary in size, so make sure there's enough room for your feet. Some of the scooters made for tricks have larger boards so that you can shift your footing more easily.

Today's kick scooters all have the same look and feel. Some have mini shock absorbers for a smoother ride. All have a brake to help stop the two-wheeler.

Are you going to be commuting on this scooter? If so, remember that you may be carrying a backpack or other heavy objects. Every scooter has a weight rating—check to make sure it can handle you and whatever you're carrying around.

Test-Ride It!

You should test-ride the scooter if at all possible. Try turning, steering, and stopping. Make sure it responds well and that you feel comfortable. Each brand handles differently, so you just need to find the one you like.

Check the brakes. Kick scooters use a rear friction brake—you press down on a panel over the rear wheel to slow or stop the scooter. Other types have hand brakes attached to the handlebars. Decide which one you like more.

Wheels

Most scooters have 100-millimeter (diameter) wheels. The Titan uses 125-millimeter wheels, so it has a higher top speed. The Xootr uses 180-millimeter wheels! Larger wheels help you go more quickly, but they take longer to build up speed. They don't maneuver quite as well, however, so you need to decide if speed or agility is more important. Larger wheels give a smoother ride, though, since they can handle cracks in road, pebbles, and other surface problems.

Kick scooter wheels are made of polyurethane rubber. They grip the pavement and sidewalk well, and they are very durable.

Brands

Since many companies produce kick scooters now, it helps to

Scooter Safety

This is a good time to go over the most important aspect of safety while riding and hitting tricks on scooters. The best thing you can do for your safety is to wear pads (discussed in chapter 4). While riding a scooter, you'll likely fall many times. Falling is a part of learning in any vehicle sport, especially while learning to do tricks. Scooter riders that appear in this book all wear pads and a helmet.

The scooter crowd knows safety is important, but being able to move their legs and arms is equally important when doing tricks. Riders wear their pads beneath their shirts and pants so that they get the most from their arms and legs. You can put your pads outside your shirt and pants, but beware that they will restrict your quickness when you may need it most.

know who the most popular manufacturers are and what they produce. This is a quick rundown—it's not a complete list, but it does cover the most common brands.

Razor Rollerboard Scooter

This was the scooter that started the current trend, and it's still one of the most popular around. Razor scooters are made by JD Corporation in Taiwan and sold through The Sharper Image. They have several different models now, but all of them share the following features:

- Wheels: 100 mm (4 inches)
- Bearings: ABEC 5
- Brakes: Rear wheel-cover friction brake

- Frame: Aluminum (with a stainless steel platform base)
- Maximum weight of rider: 220 lb. (100 kg)
- Single-action folding and unfolding
- Foldable handlebars
- Measures 21" (53 cm) long and weighs 6 lbs., folds to 4" x 12" x 21"

Kick Inline Scooter

Produced by ZAP, this scooter is a few inches taller than the Razor and built entirely of steel. It's heavier than the Razor, but can handle a little more weight and a little more punishment.

- Height: 38" (96.5 cm), 6.5" (16.5 cm) folded
- Wheelbase: 21" (53 cm)
- Weight: 9 lb. (4 kg)
- Grips: Comfort foam
- Frame: 10/20 hi-tensile steel, with powder coat color
- Wheels: Graphite, 100 mm, hi-density urethane, with sealed bearings
- Brake: Rear compression brake (chromed)
- Supports up to 250 lb. (113 kg)

Xootr

Xootr (pronounced "zooter") is produced by Nova Cruz products. Each Xootr is hand-built, and many riders consider the Xootr to be the best-quality scooter on the market. It is also the most expensive. Xootrs come in several different models, with some built for street (trick) use and others built for commuting and casual riding.

K2 Kickboard

The K2 Kickboard is a high-tech hybrid (combination) between a skateboard and scooter. It's made from aluminum, carbon, and wood, and has three wheels (one in front, two in back).

- Frame: Injected molded aluminum
- Finish: Pearl polished aluminum
- Deck: 44-cm wood-fiberglass construction with no-slip grip tape
- Wheels: 100-mm urethane wheels standard bearing ABEC 5
- Steering rod: Aluminum telescopic tube with a ball grip
- Steering mechanics: Patented steering knuckle control with tight spring and stainless steel bar
- Brake: Guard-step brake

Know-Ped (Push-Ped)

The Know-Ped, built by Patmont Motor Werks, is extremely popular. Patmont is constantly developing new models, working to create lighter versions with greater strength. The current version weighs 12 pounds (5.4 kg), can carry up to 400 pounds (181 kg), has a rear-wheel fender brake and a front caliper brake (one of the few scooters to come with dual brakes), and has folding handlebars for greater portability.

Diggler OMS Pro

This non-foldable push scooter is built specifically for off-road riding. It has 2.25-inch (57 mm) fat tires, front and rear pull brakes, an aluminum top deck, a built-in jib plate, and a suspension fork with coil spring and elastomers.

- Frame: Diggler made from .083 TIG welded 4130 Cro-Moly w/ 6mm drop outs

Personalizing Your Scooter

Most kick scooters come with only the frame and board, the wheels, the brakes, and the handlebar grips. But you can modify your scooter, both to increase its performance and to make it look cooler. Below is a list of the most common parts of the scooter that are modified. If you decide to buy any of these, check to make sure they're compatible with the scooter you own. Also, your best bet is to have the modifications made at the store before you take the scooter home.

Decks: Decks come in a wide variety of materials and sizes, though the most popular are aluminum.

Grindplates: These are attached to the underside of your board and give you a smooth surface for grinding (sliding on curbs and ledges). Without a grindplate, you'll wind up grinding the bottom of your board and will damage it after a short while.

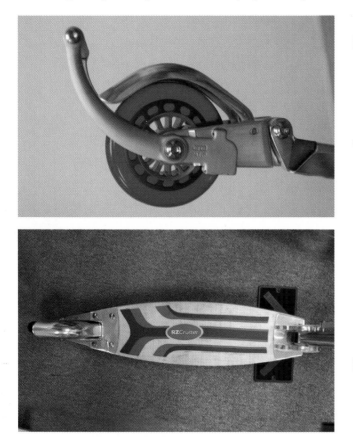

Brake extensions *(top)* and extra-wide boards *(bottom)* are two of the modifications done on kick scooters.

Handlebars: The original handlebars can be replaced with bars that angle towards you for easier reach and better control.

Grip tape: Grip tape is a durable tape with graphite dust embedded on the top. Grip tape gives you extra traction for when you do tricks. It comes in a variety of colors and patterns, and can even be bought with company logos on it.

Forks: The fork is the part of the frame that connects to the front wheel. Basic models have a simple fork to hold the wheel in place, while more advanced scooters have suspension forks with springs to absorb shock. You can purchase new forks with better suspension—some also come with new brake systems. Forks can be dual-sided or one-sided (they have springs on either one or both sides).

Pegs: Pegs are small sockets that can be added to the front and rear wheels (depending on your scooter's design). They increase the variety of tricks possible, because you can stand on the pegs while shifting your scooter. Pegs are most useful for wheelies. Pegs are usually either 9/16" (13 mm) or 2-3/4"(69 mm) long, and about 1-1/4" (31.75 mm) in diameter.

Accessories

As with bikes, you can buy a lot of different accessories for your scooter. Some of them are silly, some of them are extremely useful, and some of them are just for fun. Unlike modifications, you can add and remove accessories whenever you want. This makes the number and kind of accessories you own just a question of what you think might be nice to have and how much you're willing to spend. Some examples of accessories include a tote bag, headlights, endlights, water bottle, scooter bell, and wheelie bar.

Chapter 2

Getting Started

Before getting on your kick scooter, put on your helmet, elbow pads, and knee pads (see chapter 4 for a full description of each). Once you have your safety gear on, it's time to ride! Grab the handlebars, face forward and place your left foot on the scooter deck (board). Keep your right foot on the ground until your left feels comfortable and you have a sense of balance. You can reverse your foot position if it feels more comfortable having the right foot on the deck. Getting your stance right is important for being comfortable when riding. Once you have your stance figured out, learn the other skills in this chapter to make your scooter riding come together.

Stance

You need to find a good spot on the scooter. Don't stand too close to the handlebars—that puts too much weight in the front and not enough in the back. If you hit a bump you could go flying forward, over the handlebars. Likewise, you don't want to stand too far back. This position makes it hard to grip the handlebars. You won't be able to steer as easily or respond as quickly. Find a spot where your arms are comfortable and relaxed.

Kicking

Your kick gives you your power and speed. A good kicking technique saves energy while keeping your speed. A bad technique can throw you off balance or cause you to crash.

Different people kick differently. Some prefer short, quick kicks. Others like to swing their leg

Find your comfort zone before riding your kick scooter. Always look ahead of where you ride, not down at the wheels.

1. Push off with your left foot (or right—whichever foot is on the ground). Now start kicking the ground to build up speed. Keep your weight on your supporting leg, rather than on the kicking leg.

17

2. Your foot should touch the ground beside the footboard, back behind your supporting foot. This position gives you the best power off the push while keeping your balance.

You also want your foot to hit the ground close to the footboard—if your kick is wide you'll wind up wasting energy, and you won't be able to control the scooter as easily.

back and forth, like a pendulum, kicking the ground whenever it swings back. Others go for a few long kicks, with their leg held still in-between. Try each style to see which one feels more comfortable to you.

If you are going up a hill, you should shorten your kicks and kick more frequently. That's because you can't build momentum as easily, so you can't afford to sit and glide the way you can on a flat surface.

Riding

Riding a scooter is a matter of keeping your balance and steering. Use your stance to find the balance needed while moving before you start riding down streets.

1. Push off and kick until you're at a moderate speed.

2. Bring your kicking foot onto the board, just behind your supporting leg. Both feet should be pointing forward. Some people like to turn sideways just a little so that their weight is distributed diagonally along the footboard.

3. Keep your eyes forward to maintain balance. Don't look down at your feet to try and position them. Let the feel of your feet on the board determine their best position.

When you come to the bottom of a hill, let your scooter slow back down to your normal kicking speed before kicking again. That way you won't jolt when your foot touches the ground; if the scooter is moving faster than normal, your foot will act as a brake instead and can make you lurch a bit.

Steering

Scooters are very easy to steer. You steer them as you would a bicycle.

1. Turn the handlebars in the direction you want to go, and the front wheel will follow.

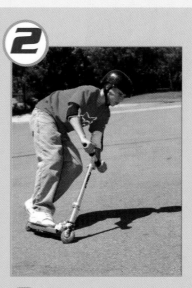

2. When you turn, lean into the turn slightly to keep your weight centered.

Braking

You have three options for stopping your scooter. The first is just to stop kicking and let the scooter slow to a halt. The second is to drag your kicking foot along the ground until you stop. The third is to use the scooter's own brake, which is either a rear friction brake over the back wheel or a front caliper (squeeze) brake controlled by a lever on the handlebar.

Always stand firmly on the footboard when braking. Jumping or hopping can cause the scooter's rear end to swing about, which might topple it—and you—to the ground. If you have a front brake, shift your feet back on the deck and bend your knees so that your weight is as far back and down as possible. If your scooter has a rear brake, you need to allow more time to stop—these brakes are more gradual, though they're also less likely to skid. Just put your kick foot on the flat part of the fender and press down firmly.

Landing

If you're doing jumps, you may find that you're hitting hard every time you come back down. Try this technique to soften your landings.

1. When you jump, bring your legs up toward your chest. This will increase your distance and height.

2. When your scooter hits the ground, bend your legs to absorb the shock of the landing.

Bailing Out

Sometimes you'll lose control of your scooter, especially when you're still new to riding it on different surfaces and going up and down hills. This is especially likely if you're doing tricks. If you do lose control, you may need to bail out. There is an easy way to bail out so that you avoid falling.

1. Lift one leg off the scooter. Also lift the hand that is on the same side as the leg you have just lifted.

2. Use your free hand to balance yourself as you step onto the ground in a running motion.

3. Use your hand that's still holding onto the handlebars to turn the scooter away from the direction in which you have stepped off. Now you can safely stop your momentum.

If you're going too fast and bailing can't be done quick enough, simply let go of the scooter and leap clear—better for it to fall and for you to fall away from it than for it to fall on you.

Basic tricks

Now that you know how to ride, it's time to learn some tricks. The following tricks are the three most basic tricks to get you started.

Ollie

The ollie is the first trick you need to learn if you want to start trick riding. Don't confuse it with the skateboarding trick—that is where the name comes from, but this is a different technique. Fortunately, it's still simple.

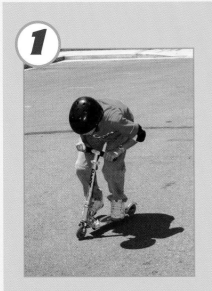

1. Place your feet evenly on your board. Jump up and pull your scooter up in the air with you.

2. Use the handlebars to pull the scooter up. Keep your feet on the scooter at all times.

3 Ollie (continued)

3. Land with your feet on the board. Remember to bend your knees to absorb the shock.

Bunny Hop

A bunny hop uses the same jumping technique as an ollie. The difference in the bunny hop is that you are only using the back wheel for the jump and the landing. Most people do bunny hops with one foot on the brake, but you can do it with your feet evenly placed instead.

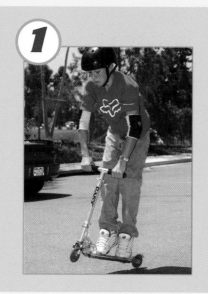

1. Ollie and pull up hard on the handlebars so the front wheel rises higher than the back.

2. Crouch down while still in mid-air.

3. Land on the back wheel first, then let the front come forward and touch down.

Pogo

This trick is great for learning to balance on your scooter. It can also be used to jump stairs, once you're good at it.

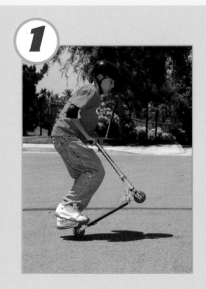

1. Stand with one foot on your back wheel and the other foot either on the board or in the air.

2 Pogo (continued)

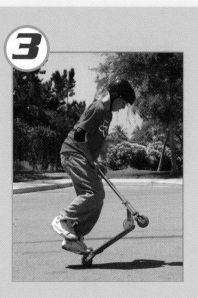

2. Now ollie and try to get as much air as you can.

3. As soon as you land, ollie again. Repeat steps 2 and 3 until finished.

You can try to land a pogo in the same place every time, or move forward or backward. You can also pogo side to side. Each variation is just a matter of shifting your weight as you ollie, and of tugging the handlebar so that the scooter is in the desired location before it starts to fall back down.

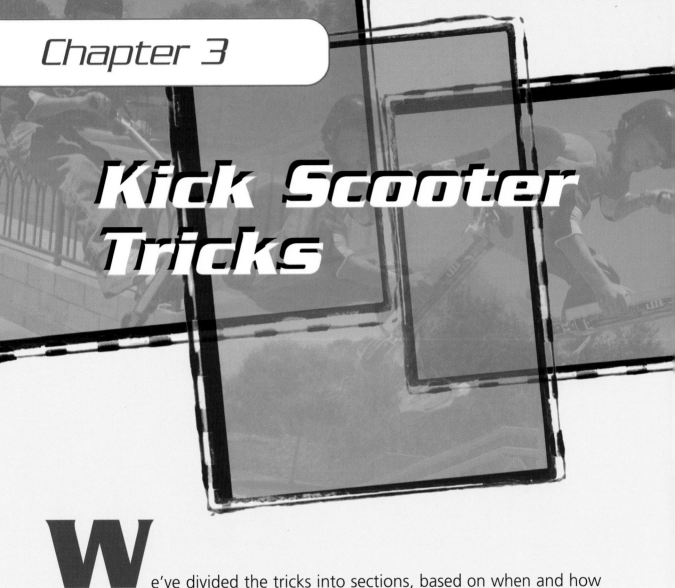

Kick Scooter Tricks

We've divided the tricks into sections, based on when and how you perform them. Some of them actually fit in several categories, but it might be easier to think of them this way—as you gain more practice you can experiment, trying tricks at different times and in different ways. You may even come up with some tricks of your own.

Ground Tricks

These are tricks that start on the ground and which don't need any ramps or obstacles to complete them. Any flat surface will do for ground tricks.

Manual

A manual is a wheelie that you hold. The key to riding great manuals is, of course, balance. Balancing your kick scooter takes lots of practice, but don't give up. Manuals are cool tricks to show off on your block.

Sometimes you can do a manual into a trick. Some tricks you can come out of into a manual. These are both advanced tricks, and you should perfect all your tricks before trying to combine them.

1. Push off and kick forward slowly. Put your deck foot at the back and your kick foot on the rear fender (or the brake).

2. Bend your back a little and pull up on the handlebars. Keep your momentum by leaning your body forward. You won't go very far since you're standing on the brake, but with practice you can keep this in the air for a while.

Nose Manual

The nose manual is a front-wheel wheelie. Once you master this trick you can move on to a wide variety of others. Be careful! The nose manual is tricky, and you'll fall several times before you master it. Be sure to wear all your safety gear.

1. Glide forward at a moderate speed with your feet one behind the other (or side by side) on the deck. Do NOT squeeze the brakes.

2. Lean forward a little and lift your rear wheel off the ground. Use your forward weight to help pull the rear wheel up. Once the wheel is in the air, squeeze your brakes lightly (quick taps) to keep the rear up.

One Footer

This is one of the most basic jumping tricks. Before you try it, however, make sure you can jump and land cleanly.

1. Glide forward at a comfortable speed and launch off a ramp (or ollie from the flat pavement).

2. Just before you hit the highest point of the jump, pull one of your feet off the board and kick to the side. Don't kick forward or backward—it'll throw off your scooter. Hold your foot out as long as you feel comfortable.

3. Pull your foot back in and try to set it back on the deck before you land.

No-Footer

Before you try a no-footer, make sure you can jump and land consistently.

1. Glide at a comfortable speed and launch off a ramp (or ollie from the flat pavement).

2. At the height of the jump, push down on the handlebars. Kick your feet out to the sides (your weight should be on the handlebars).

3. Pull your legs back in and set your feet back on the deck before you land.

Air Tricks

The following tricks can only work when you're in the air. For example, you can do a no-footer on the ground, but for an x-up or an x-grab you really need to be airborne.

X-Up

The x-up is a fairly simple trick as long as you know how to ollie well.

1. Ollie or launch off a ramp as high as you can.

2. At the peak of your jump, twist your handlebars clockwise as far as they'll go. Your arms will form an X.

3. Turn the handlebar back to normal and land.

Once you've mastered the x-up, you can even try it one-handed: ollie, take one hand off the bars, turn them with the other hand, turn them back, and then grab the bars with your free hand again before you land.

X-Grab

This is basically an x-up with a grab thrown in. The trick here is to mind your balance while you're doing this so you don't fall off the scooter.

1. Ollie or launch off a ramp and do an x-up.

2. With your arms still crossed in an X, crouch and grab the bottom of your scooter with your inside hand.

3. Let go, straighten up, and grab the handlebars again before you land.

4 X-Grab (continued)

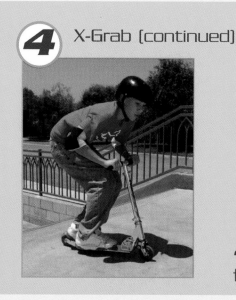

4. Turn the handlebar back to face forward and land.

Boardslide

This is the basic slide. Just make sure you wax the object you're planning to slide on. Use a candle for a curb or concrete ledge. Boardsliding without first waxing the surface can tear up your scooter or, worse, make you jerk to a stop and fall off.

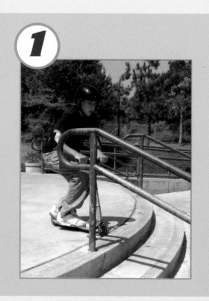

1. Glide alongside the object at a comfortable speed.

2

3

2. Ollie and rotate your scooter ninety degree so you can land on the bottom of your deck. You don't want to land on your wheels. Keep your shoulders facing toward the direction you are sliding.

3. Slide along the object. Your momentum should carry you along.

4

4. When you slow down or come to the end, bounce or ollie up and turn ninety degrees to face forward. Land on your wheels and ride forward.

Chapter 4

Safety Gear and Scooter Maintenance

As with any sport, riding a scooter can be dangerous. You're moving at a relatively high speed, and there's nothing but a thin platform between you and the ground. You'll fall down quite a few times, especially if you're doing tricks, so be prepared.

Helmet

Always wear a helmet. Head injuries are serious, and you don't have to be moving fast to cause serious damage when you fall. Helmets come in a variety of colors and patterns, so you'll be able to find one that fits your image and style. Make sure you buy a helmet approved by either the American National Standards Institute (ANSI), the Snell Memorial Foundation, the Canadian Standards Association (CSA), or the American Society for Testing and Materials

(ASTM). Don't get a helmet that doesn't have an approval from at least one of those organizations displayed on its packaging.

Equally important to owning and wearing a helmet is how it fits on your head. Your helmet should be snug enough that it won't come off, but not so tight that it hurts. It should sit firmly on your head but not obstruct your vision in any way. If you skateboard or bike, you can use the same helmet.

Shoes

Footing is very important on a scooter. You need to make sure you're wearing well-made, durable shoes with good traction. Sneakers and other athletic shoes work well. Your shoes should stay on your feet and be comfortable. Avoid shoes with heels, dress shoes, or sandals.

Helmets worn by skateboarders and cyclists are equally good for kick scooter riding. Wear durable athletic shoes that have good traction on the soles.

Knee and Elbow Pads

The best knee and elbow pads are made of lightweight foam covered in nylon. Knee and elbow pads use Velcro straps to fit around the joints snugly. The straps should be tight enough to hold, but not so tight that they cut into your leg or arm—or cut off your circulation. For added protection, buy pads that have a hard plastic cap that covers the point of the elbow or knee.

Gloves

If you fall, you'll probably try to catch yourself with your hands. That's a normal reaction, but it could leave you with some nasty scrapes. Wearing gloves will protect your hands from most falls. Your fingers shouldn't slide around inside them, and you should still be able to maintain a good grip on the handlebars. Leather is a good choice, since it's durable, but even cloth gloves are better than nothing.

Wrist Guards

Using your hands to catch yourself during a fall can easily jerk your hands back on your wrists. This can cause a severe sprain. Wrist guards prevent your wrists from bending all the way back. You can get them in cool colors and patterns, and the first time you land on your hands you'll be glad you bought them.

A good pair of gloves will cover your fingers and wrap around your wrists. Elbow pads are easy to slap on and off. After your first fall, you'll be glad you're wearing both.

Competitions

Kick scooter riding is just beginning to catch on as a recognized sport. Only a handful of competitions existed at the time of this book's writing. Most competitions are in Europe, sponsored by IKSA (the International Kicksled and Scooter Association). The Eurocup races are open to any scooter athlete (of any nationality) who has taken part in at least five Eurocup events. The jury for a race is selected by the event organizer and the four nations with the most participants, each selecting a single jury member. Any type of kick or push scooter can be used. They cannot have any motors, gears, sails, or sharp edges which could injure other competitors.

Dress for Success

Wear clothing that's loose enough for easy movement when you ride, but not so baggy it could get caught on the handlebars or in the wheels. Wearing bell-bottomed jeans that cover your feet is just asking for trouble. If you're wearing long sleeves, you might want to roll them up above your elbow to avoid the risk of catching a cuff on the handle or the brake.

Scooter Maintenance and Safety

It's important to keep your scooter in working order. Regular tightening of bolts will prevent breakdowns of wheels and handlebars. If you do a lot of tricks on your scooter, you need to also check for wear damage. Your scooter will suffer scrapes and gouges from hard riding and trick practice. Look for bent wheel housings, bent forks, and a bent deck. Each

Wheels and hubs come in different colors and styles. You can mix and match to suit your own flair and style.

of these problems can cause poor riding and handling, which can cause injury.

Maybe the greatest wear your scooter will suffer is to its wheels. The urethane wheels get beat up on the rough streets and sidewalks on which you ride. If you ride frequently, you can plan to change your wheels at least once a year. There is an easy step-by-step plan that any rider can learn to change his or her own scooter wheels.

Changing Wheels

Always fold your scooter before changing a wheel.

1. You'll need two 5-mm Allen wrenches.
2. Hold the axle-bolt on one side of the fork by one Allen wrench and at the same time unscrew the axle-bolt on the other side with the other wrench.
3. Take the wheel out. If the new wheel comes with bearings, skip to Step 4. If not, you'll need to do the following:

   • Use a wrench and a hammer to remove the bearings and spacer from the old wheel. Be careful not to damage the bearings.

   • Slide the bearings into the new wheel's axle and make sure the spacer is in position. The bolts should be able to go through the axle. Use the hammer to fit the bearings to the new wheel.

4. Replace the wheel.
5. Screw the axle-bolts back on. It's easiest to do this when the wheel is in a horizontal position.
6. Make sure the wheel is firmly fastened.

Safety Check

Riding your scooter should be fun, but you need to stay safe, too. Getting hurt isn't fun for anyone, and it could keep you from riding until you heal. So before you ride, follow these six quick steps:

1. Check your scooter. Make sure the wheels spin freely and the steering turns easily. Make sure the folding mechanism is locked up and the locking pins for the handlebars are in place.
2. Always wear your safety gear, especially your helmet.
3. When riding, watch out for other people and especially for cars when you're crossing a road. Cars move a lot faster than you do and can't stop as easily.
4. Don't ride when it's wet out—your brakes won't work and your wheels will skid.
5. If you're riding at night, make sure you have reflective stripes or lights on your scooter and that your helmet has reflectors as well.
6. Don't try a trick you aren't ready for or a hill that's too steep for you.

Hitting the Streets

Now that you have the building blocks for scooter fun, tricks, and safety, its time for you to get your gear on and hit the streets. The friendly competition is there for you to practice and improve. A pogo here, an ollie there, are just moments away.

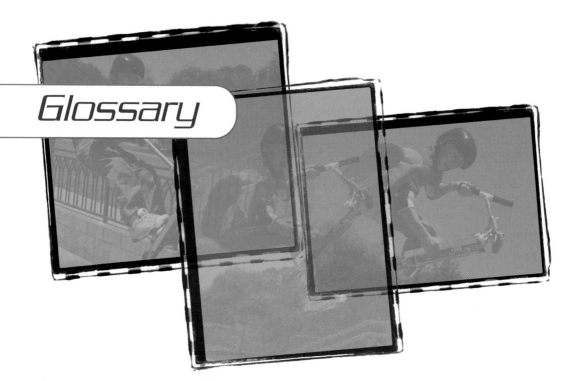

Glossary

air Getting a scooter off the ground. Any time you jump or ollie, you are getting some air.

bail Stopping your scooter or leaping away from it when a trick goes wrong, to save yourself from injury.

Go-Ped The brand name of products produced by Patmont Motor Werks, including the Know-Ped. Also used specifically for their gas-powered scooters.

kick scooter A scooter that moves by its rider kicking the ground to build up speed and momentum.

Know-Ped A human-powered, two-wheeled folding kick scooter produced by Patmont. Sometimes used to refer to any folding kick scooter.

push scooter Same as a kick scooter.

Razor A folding kick scooter created by JD Corporation in Taiwan. Often used to refer to any folding kick scooter.

For More Information

International Human Powered Vehicle Assocation (IHPVA)

P.O. Box 1307
San Luis Obispo, CA 93406-1307
(877) 333-1029
Web site: http://www.ihpva.org

International Kicksled and Scooter Association (IKSA)

Thijza Brouwer
Kl. Benninkstraat 19
8281 ZV Genemuiden
The Netherlands
+31-6-538-69770
e-mail: naf@autoped.nl
Web site: http://www.iksaworld.com

For Further Reading

Case, Jeremy, and Zac Sandler. *Scooter Mania*. New York: Penguin, 2000.

Case, Jeremy, and Zac Sandler. *Scooters! The Ultimate Guide to the Coolest Ride!* New York: Aladdin, 2001.

Schlesinger, Willy, et al. *Scooter Mania!: Fun Tricks and Cool Tips for Today's Hottest Ride.* New York: St. Martin's Press, 2000.

Sharpe, Ben, and Paul Cemmick. *The Ultimate Scooter Guide.* New York: Scholastic, 2001.

Williams, Vera B. *Scooter*. New York: Harper Collins, 2000.

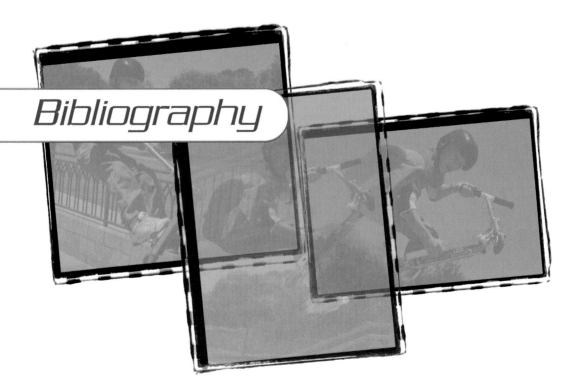

Bibliography

Allen, Frederick E. "Behind the Cutting Edge: The New Time Travel."
American Heritage, Volume 53, Number 2. April/May 2002.

Bellis, Mary. "The History of Scooters." Retrieved March 24, 2002
(http://inventors.about.com/library/inventors/blscooter.htm).

Chiu, Danny. "You've Seen the Scooter . . . Now Follow the Sport!" *Market
News Express*. Retrieved March 23, 2002 (http://www.tdctrade.com/mne/
toy/010102.htm).

Davis, Phil. "Razor Scooters—Zooming Straight to the Emergency
Room?"Retrieved March 3, 2002 (http://www.eref.net/sports_recreation/
features/scooter_safety.asp).

Dutch Autoped Federation. Retrieved March 25, 2002 (http://www.autoped.nl/
home.htm).

Edge Sports, Inc. Retrieved March 25, 2002 (http://www.edgesports.net/
html/safety_gear.html).

Fry, Kathie. "How to Buy a Razor Scooter." Retrieved March 23, 2002
(http://inlineskating.about.com/library/weekly/aa-scooter-razor-buying.htm).

"How to Ride a Kick Scooter." Ehow.com. Retrieved March 25, 2002
(http://www.ehow.com/ehow/ehow.jsp?id=18561).

IKSA World (International Kicksled and Scooter Association). Retrieved March 25, 2002 (http://www.iksaworld.com).

JD Corporation. Retrieved March 23, 2002 (http://www.razor-scooter.com).

RadScooter. Retrieved March 23, 2002 (http://radscooter.iwarp.com).

Razor Scooter Tricks. Retrieved March 23, 2002 (http://communities.msn.co.uk/razorscootertricks/razorscootertricks.msnw).

Scooter Info. Sponsored by Nova Cruz, the manufacturer of Xootr scooters. Retrieved March 4, 2002 (http://www.scooter-info.com).

Scooter Village. Retrieved March 5, 2002 (http://www.scootervillage.com).

Scooterz. Retrieved March 25, 2002 (http://www.maxpages.com/loganspage/scooterz).

ScootHead. Retrieved March 26, 2002 (http://www.scoothead.com).

Index

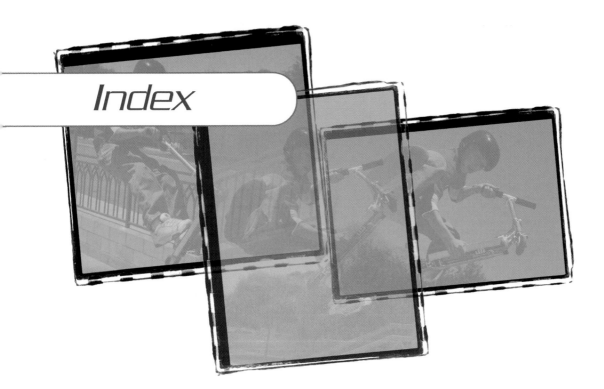

About the Author

Aaron Rosenberg was born in New Jersey, grew up in New Orleans, and now lives in New York. He has taught college English, has worked in corporate graphics, and now runs his own roleplaying game publishing company (www.clockworksgames.com). He has written short stories, essays, poems, articles, novels, and roleplaying games.

Acknowledgments

Thanks to Nathan Reid of Team Razor.

Credits

Cover, pp. 9, 10, 11, 14, 17–26, 28–35, 37, 38, 40 © Tony Donaldson/Icon SMI/Rosen Publishing; pp. 4–5 © Carl Schneider/Corbis; p. 7 © Hulton-Deutsch Collection/Corbis; p. 8 © AP/Wide World Photos.

Editor

Mark Beyer

Design and Layout

Les Kanturek